Silence
Transformed
into Life

The Testament of His Final Year

Silence
Transformed
into Life

John Paul II

New City Press
Hyde Park, New York

Published in the United States by New City Press
202 Cardinal Rd., Hyde Park, NY 12538
www.newcitypress.com
©2006 New City Press

English translation used with permission
© Libreria Editrice Vaticana

Selection of texts based on *I giorni del silenzio*
©2005 Città Nuova, Rome, Italy

Cover design by Durva Correia

Library of Congress Cataloging-in-Publication Data:

John Paul II, Pope, 1920-2005
  [Giorni del silenzio. English]
  Silence transformed into life : the testament of his final year / John
Paul II.
    v. cm.
  Contents: Do not be afraid -- Open wide the doors to Christ -- I
looked for you; now you've come to see me and for this I thank you
-- Totus tuus -- Amen.
  ISBN-13: 978-1-56548-237-1 (alk. paper)
  ISBN-10: 1-56548-237-9 (alk. paper)
  1. Christian life--Catholic authors. 2. Love--Religious aspects
--Catholic Church. 3. Suffering--Religious aspects--Catholic Church.
I. Title
BX2350.3.J613 2006
248.4'82--dc22
                                          20050262778

Nihil Obstat: Rev. Michael F. Hull
Imprimatur: Bishop Robert A. Brucato, Vicar General
            Archdiocese of New York   September 20, 2005

Printed in the United States of America

Contents

Foreword 7

Do Not Be Afraid 11

Open Wide the Doors to Christ 49

You've Come to See Me,
   and I Thank You 79

Totus Tuus 93

Amen 109

Spiritual Testament. 125

Foreword

Karol Wojtyla lived through the last eight decades of the twentieth century, a time marked by technological progress and brilliant scientific discoveries, but also by unprecedented poverty, holocausts, bombs, and terror. Nevertheless, he did not succumb to existential pessimism. His youthful voice re-echoes, "All are called to holiness, and holy people alone can renew humanity" (p. 27). Whence came this David who, when the rest of us were cowering before Goliath, so to speak, shone with the light of Christ? God often chooses his people's leaders when they are young. Samuel was inspired to anoint as King David, Jesse's youngest son. John Paul II also felt a call early in life. One anecdote from his youth tells how he awoke to find his father praying in the Polish fashion, flat on his face, his arms stretched out like a cross. Young Karol felt Christ's powerful presence in the room, a presence that he intuited the whole world really longs for. This sense never left him.

He opened his pontificate telling the world not to be afraid. "Open wide the doors to Christ!" He did not proclaim, "Follow me!" but "Follow Christ!" We still feel that call. He summoned the youth in particular to bring a fresh breath of optimism to the world through their personal choices of mature faith. He insisted that evil will never have the last word (cf. p. 44). He teaches us to confront evil with the simple weapons of love, and to have confidence in Christ working through us. Christ is Truth. On the long and grueling journey towards truth, reason alone does not suffice. We tend to let ourselves be caged up into our own thoughts. John Paul invites us to unlock the door to contemplation, to fix our gaze on Jesus, and communicate his words of hope and salvation to all people of good will. He never stops reminding us of the divine gifts of freedom, of essential human dignity, of courage. His clear, unequivocal message sounded even throughout his last year, as you will find in the first half of this anthology.

This volume also includes selections from the last year of his life that call for a more open society, for "civic reasonableness [that] recognizes universal human rights" (p. 19). Even as he was dying, he continued teaching us how to listen to our neighbor's cry for help, to build bridges and to listen to one another, to share each other's gifts. As he thanked the Jews and Muslims who wanted to come and pray with him in the hospital, he showed us how to see our neighbor not as an enemy to be fought but as a potential friend (cf. p. 29).

Karol Wojtyla lived what he spoke. One section in this collection treats of how to cope with physical suffering. Christ, God who came to share our existence, gave us one commandment — to love. Jesus desires our genuine happiness. Love triumphs even in the abyss of suffering. In our sufferings we can be privileged cooperators with Christ. John Paul calls us to the mystery of joy with Mary beside us united to the cross, helping us to fulfill God's will in every moment of life. He begs Mary to teach us to stand with practical love, involved in giving help. Only in suffering do we learn humility, to work together for the dawn of the civilization of love. All Christians together must build up the world, starting from within the depths of silence and of prayer, in a fraternal spirit, to give an account of the hope that is in us, trusting in people's goodness and in the Father.

In his Spiritual Testament, John Paul II reminds us how much the mutual love of his kindred in blood and spirit have helped him. They reinforced his devotion to God and to the fulfillment of the divine plan. With them he lived the "spirituality of communion" which he urges us to emulate.

In solidarity with the throngs who continue to pay homage to his mortal remains at the Basilica of St. Peter, it is appropriate that we treasure the last words of a person who has been our father, our brother, our friend. Using this book to consult the map so to speak, we can keep our eye on the never failing compass of his advice.

Julian Stead, O.S.B.

Do Not Be Afraid

Do not be afraid: God will always be with you! With his help you will be able to find the paths that lead to the heart of every person.

Homily, 2 May 2004

Dear friends, I ask the Lord to be a witness of hope among you, a witness of that hope which "does not disappoint," because it is founded on God's love "poured into our hearts through the Holy Spirit who has been given to us" (Rom 5:5). Today, the world is especially in need of an extra measure of hope!

Homily, 6 June 2004

D o not be afraid of being opposed by the world! Jesus has assured us, "I have conquered the world!" (Jn 16:33).

Do not be afraid even of your own weakness and inadequacy! ... Communicate the message of Christ's hope, grace and love, keeping always alive, in this passing world, the eternal perspective of heaven.

Apostolic Letter
The Rapid Development
24 January 2005

Ten years ago, in *Tertio Millennio Adveniente* (10 November 1994), I had the joy of proposing to the Church a program of preparation for the *Great Jubilee of the Year 2000.* It seemed to me that this historic moment presented itself as a great grace. I realized, of course, that a simple chronological event, however evocative, could not by itself bring about great changes. Unfortunately the millennium began with events which were in tragic continuity with the past, and often with its worst aspects. A scenario emerged which, despite certain positive elements, is marred by acts of violence and bloodshed which cause continued concern. Even so, in inviting the Church to celebrate the Jubilee of the two-thousandth anniversary of the Incarnation, I was convinced — and I still am, more than ever! — that this celebration would be of benefit to humanity in the long term.

Apostolic Letter
Mane nobiscum Domine (I, 6)
7 October 2004

There is another challenge that I wish to mention: *the challenge of freedom*. All of you know how important this is to me, especially because of the history of my native people....

Freedom is a great good, because only by freedom can human beings find fulfillment in a manner befitting their nature. Freedom is like light. It enables us to choose responsibly our proper goals and the right means of achieving them.

> Address to the Diplomatic Corps
> Accredited to the Holy See
> 10 January 2005

There need be no fear that legitimate religious freedom would limit other freedoms or be injurious to the life of civil society. On the contrary, together with religious freedom, all other freedoms develop and thrive, inasmuch as freedom is an indivisible good, the prerogative of the human person and his dignity.

Address to the Diplomatic Corps
Accredited to the Holy See
10 January 2005

In our society, characterized by the global phenomenon of migration, individuals must seek the proper balance between respect for their own identity and recognition of that of others....

We should encourage a mutual fertilization of cultures. This presumes knowledge and openness between cultures in an atmosphere of true understanding and goodwill.... It will be necessary to combine the principle of respect for cultural differences with the protection of values that are common and inalienable because they are founded on universal human rights. This gives rise to that climate of civic reasonableness which permits friendly and peaceful coexistence.

World Day of Migrants
and Refugees, 2005

The image from the Prophet Isaiah, to which I have several times referred at the meetings with the youth of the whole world (cf. Is 21:11–12), could also be used here to invite all believers to be "morning watchmen." As such, Christians must above all listen to the cry for help that comes from so many migrants and refugees, but they must then foster, with active commitment, prospects of hope that will herald the dawn of a more open and supportive society. It is up to them in the first place to discern God's presence in history, even when everything still seems to be enveloped in darkness.

World Day of Migrants
and Refugees, 2005

Indeed, much of the violence that humanity suffers in our times is rooted in misunderstanding as well as in rejection of the values and identity of foreign cultures. Many times such situations could be overcome through a better knowledge of each other.

25th World Day of Tourism
27 September 2004

Contact with others leads to discovering their secret, to being open to them in order to recognize their good qualities and thus contribute to a better knowledge of each one. This is a lengthy process that aims to shape societies and cultures, making them more and more a reflection of the multi-faceted gifts of God to human beings.

World Day of Migrants
and Refugees, 2005

Human life is a precious gift to be loved and defended in each of its stages. The Commandment, "You shall not kill," always requires respecting and promoting human life, from its beginning to its natural end. It is a command that applies even in the presence of illness and when physical weakness reduces a person's ability to be self-reliant. If growing old, with its inevitable conditions, is accepted serenely in the light of faith, it can become an invaluable opportunity for better understanding the mystery of the Cross, which gives full meaning to human existence.

Message for Lent, 2005

The greater amount of free time in the last stage of life offers the elderly an opportunity to face primary issues that perhaps had been previously ignored due to concerns that were pressing or considered a priority. Knowledge of the nearness of the final goal leads the elderly person to focus on what is essential, giving importance to those things that the passing of years does not destroy.

Precisely because of this condition, the elderly person can carry out his or her role in society. If it is true that we live upon the heritage of those who have gone before us, and that our future depends definitively on how the cultural values of our own people are transmitted to us, then the wisdom and experience of the elderly can illuminate our path on the way of progress toward an ever more complete form of civilization.

Message for Lent, 2005

It is up to you lay people to witness to the faith through your own particular virtues: fidelity and gentleness in the family, competence at work, tenacity in serving the common good, solidarity in social relations, creativity in doing useful deeds for evangelization and human promotion. It is also up to you, in close communion with the pastors, to show that the Gospel is timely and that faith does not tear the believer from history but roots him in it more deeply.

Homily, 5 September 2004

Dear Friends, I invite you to renew your "yes" and I leave you with three tasks. The *first* is *contemplation*: strive to walk on the path of holiness, keeping your gaze fixed on Jesus, the one teacher and savior of all.

The *second task* is *communion*: strive to promote the spirituality of unity with the pastors of the Church, with all the brethren in the faith and with the other ecclesial associations. Be the leaven of dialogue with all people of good will.

The *third task* is *mission:* as lay people, take the leaven of the Gospel to homes and schools, to places of work and recreation. The Gospel is a word of hope and salvation for the world.

Angelus, 5 September 2004

The Church needs genuine witnesses for the new evangelization, men and women whose lives have been transformed by meeting Jesus, men and women capable of communicating this experience to others. The Church needs saints. All are called to holiness, and holy people alone can renew humanity.

Message Prepared for the 20th World Youth Day, 6 August 2005

Overcoming evil with weapons of love becomes the way in which each person can contribute to the peace of all. Christians and believers of different religions are called to walk this path, together with those who accept the universal moral law.

Promoting peace in the world is our common mission!

Homily, 1 January 2005

May everyone see in his neighbor not an enemy to be fought, but a brother to be accepted and loved, so that we may join in building a better world.

Accueil Notre-Dame, 14 August 2004

In these days of my stay here at the Gemelli Hospital, I have been particularly aware of the presence and attention of so many people who work in the mass media. Today I want to offer them a word of thanks, for I am well aware of the sacrifices they make in carrying out their appreciated service, through which the faithful in every part of the world can feel that I am closer and can accompany me with their affection and prayers....

In this season of Lent, which is an invitation to draw more abundantly from the Word of God, I am happy to recall that it is also possible to find spiritual nourishment on the radio, television and Internet. I am grateful to those who dedicate themselves to these new forms of evangelization by taking advantage of the mass media.

Angelus, 13 March 2005

To those working in communication, especially to believers involved in this important field, I extend the invitation that from the very beginning of my ministry as pastor of the universal Church I wished to express to the entire world: "Do not be afraid!"

Do not be afraid of new technologies! These rank among the marvelous things God has placed at our disposal in order to discover, use and make known the truth.

Apostolic Letter
The Rapid Development
24 January 2005

The communications media have become so important that they are the principal means of guidance and inspiration for many people in their personal, familial, and social behavior. We are dealing with a complex problem, because this culture, prescinding from its content, arises from the very existence of new ways to communicate with hitherto unknown techniques and vocabulary....

The mass media can and must promote justice and solidarity by reporting events accurately and truthfully, analyzing situations and problems completely, and providing a forum for different opinions.

Apostolic Letter
The Rapid Development
24 January 2005

The modern technologies increase to a remarkable extent the speed, quantity and accessibility of communication, but they do not favor that delicate exchange which takes place between mind and mind, between heart and heart, and which should characterize any communication in the service of solidarity and love.

Apostolic Letter
The Rapid Development
24 January 2005

The media can teach billions of people about other parts of the world and other cultures. With good reason they have been called "the first Areopagus of the modern age ... for many the chief means of information and education, of guidance and inspiration in their behavior as individuals, families, and within society at large" (*Redemptoris Missio*, 37). Accurate knowledge promotes understanding, dispels prejudice, and awakens the desire to learn more. Images especially have the power to convey lasting impressions and to shape attitudes. They teach people how to regard members of other groups and nations, subtly influencing whether they are considered as friends or enemies, allies or potential adversaries.

Message for the 39th World
Communications Day, 24 January 2005

When others are portrayed in hostile terms, seeds of conflict are sown which can all too easily escalate into violence, war, or even genocide. Instead of building unity and understanding, the media can be used to demonize other social, ethnic and religious groups, fomenting fear and hatred. Those responsible for the style and content of what is communicated have a grave duty to ensure that this does not happen. Indeed, the media have enormous potential for promoting peace and building bridges between peoples, breaking the fatal cycle of violence, reprisal, and fresh violence that is so widespread today.

Message for the 39th World
Communications Day, 24 January 2005

As a supreme good and the condition for attaining many other essential goods, peace is the dream of every generation. Yet how many wars and armed conflicts continue to take place — between states, ethnic groups, peoples and groups living in the same territory. From one end of the world to the other, they are claiming countless innocent victims and spawning so many other evils! Our thoughts naturally turn to various countries in the Middle East, Africa, Asia, and Latin America, where recourse to arms and violence has not only led to incalculable material damage, but also fomented hatred and increased the causes of tension, thereby adding to the difficulty of finding and implementing solutions capable of reconciling the legitimate interests of all the parties involved. In addition to these tragic evils there is the brutal, inhuman phenomenon of terrorism, a scourge which has taken on a global dimension unknown to previous generations.

How can the great challenge of building peace overcome such evils?... I have spoken out and I shall continue to do so, pointing out the paths to peace and urging that they be followed with courage and patience. The arrogance of power must be countered with reason, force with dialogue, pointed weapons with outstretched hands, evil with good.

Address to the Diplomatic Corps
Accredited to the Holy See
10 January 2005

The Catholic Church, because of her universal nature, is always directly engaged in the great causes for which the men and women of our age struggle and hope. She considers herself a stranger to no people, since wherever there are Christians, the whole body of the Church is involved; indeed, wherever there is any one individual, we sense a bond of brotherhood.

Address to the Diplomatic Corps
Accredited to the Holy See
10 January 2005

No man or woman of good will can renounce the struggle to overcome evil with good. This fight can be fought effectively only with the weapons of love.

World Day of Peace, 1 January 2005

Evil is not some impersonal, deterministic force at work in the world. It is the result of human freedom. Freedom, which distinguishes human beings from every other creature on earth, is ever present at the heart of the drama of evil and is constantly associated with it. Evil always has a name and a face: the name and face of those men and women who freely choose it....

At its deepest level, evil is a tragic rejection of the demands of love.

World Day of Peace, 1 January 2005

It is necessary to resist *fear of the truth*, which can sometimes arise from the fear of offending people.

The truth, which is Christ himself (cf. Jn 8:32, 36), sets us free from every form of compromise with self-serving falsehoods.

Address to the Tribunal of the Roman Rota
29 January 2005

When, as pope, I visited the Auschwitz-Birkenau camp in 1979, I paused before the monuments dedicated to the victims. There were inscriptions in many languages: Polish, English, Bulgarian, Romany, Czech, Danish, French, Greek, Hebrew, Yiddish, Spanish, Flemish, Serbo-Croatian, German, Norwegian, Russian, Romanian, Hungarian and Italian. All these languages spoke of the victims of Auschwitz, of real, yet in many cases completely anonymous men, women and children. I paused somewhat longer before the inscription written in Hebrew. It said: "This inscription invites us to remember the people whose sons and daughters were doomed to total extermination. This people has its origin in Abraham, our father in faith (cf. Rom 4:11–12), as Paul of Tarsus has said. This, the very people that received from God the commandment, 'You shall not kill,' itself experienced in a special measure what killing means. No one is permitted to pass by this inscription with indifference."

Message on the 60th Anniversary
of the Liberation of the Prisoners
of the Auschwitz-Birkenau Death Camp
15 January 2005

No one is permitted to pass by the tragedy of the Shoah. That attempt at the systematic destruction of an entire people falls like a shadow on the history of Europe and the whole world; it is a crime which will for ever darken the history of humanity. May it serve, today and for the future, as a warning: there must be no yielding to ideologies that justify contempt for human dignity on the basis of race, color, language or religion. I make this appeal to everyone, and particularly to those who would resort, in the name of religion, to acts of oppression and terrorism.

Message on the 60th Anniversary
of the Liberation of the Prisoners
of the Auschwitz-Birkenau Death Camp
15 January 2005

In speaking of the victims of Auschwitz, I cannot fail to recall that, in the midst of that unspeakable concentration of evil, there were also heroic examples of commitment to good. Certainly there were many persons who were willing, in spiritual freedom, to endure suffering and to show love, not only for their fellow prisoners, but also for their tormentors. Many did so out of love for God and for man; others in the name of the highest spiritual values. Their attitude bore clear witness to a truth that is often expressed in the Bible: even though man is capable of evil, and at times boundless evil, evil itself will never have the last word. In the very abyss of suffering, love can triumph. The witness to this love shown in Auschwitz must never be forgotten. It must never cease to rouse consciences, resolve conflicts, inspire the building of peace.

Message on the 60th Anniversary
of the Liberation of the Prisoners
of the Auschwitz-Birkenau Death Camp
15 January 2005

Faith teaches us that even in the most difficult and painful trials — such as the disas-
ter that has struck Southeast Asia in these past
days — God never abandons us. He came, in
the mystery of Christmas, to share our existence.

The Child of Bethlehem is the One who, on
the vigil of his redeeming death, will leave to us
the commandment to love one another as he
has loved us (cf. Jn 13: 34). It is in the concrete
fulfillment of his commandment that he makes
his presence felt.

This evangelical message grounds the hope
of a better world, provided that we walk in his
love.

Angelus, 2 January 2005

45

The feast of Christmas, perhaps the dearest to popular tradition, is rich in symbols connected with the different cultures. There is no doubt that the most important of them all is the crib.

Next to the crib we find the traditional Christmas tree. This, too, is an ancient tradition that emphasizes the value of life, for in the winter season the evergreen fir becomes a sign of undying life. Christmas gifts are usually placed on the tree or arranged at its base. The symbol thus also becomes eloquent in a typically Christian sense. It calls to mind the tree of life (cf. Gn 2:9), a figure of Christ, God's supreme gift to humanity.

So the message of the Christmas tree is that life remains "ever green" if it becomes a gift — not so much of material things, but of oneself, in friendship and sincere affection, in fraternal help and forgiveness, in time shared and in listening to one another.

Angelus, 19 December 2004

Christ is born for us:
come, let us adore him!
On this solemn day we come to you,
tender Babe of Bethlehem.
By your birth you have hidden your divinity
in order to share our frail human nature.
In the light of faith, we acknowledge you
as *true God*, *made man* out of love for us.
You alone are the Redeemer of mankind!

Before the crib where you lie helpless,
let there be an end to *the spread of violence*
in its many forms,
the source of untold suffering;
let there be an end to the numerous
situations of unrest
which risk degenerating into open conflict;
let there arise a firm will to *seek peaceful solutions*,
respectful of the legitimate aspirations
of individuals and peoples.

Babe of Bethlehem, prophet of peace,
encourage attempts to promote
dialogue and *reconciliation*,
sustain the *efforts to build peace*,
which hesitantly, yet not without hope,
are being made
to bring about a more tranquil
present and future for so many
of our brothers and sisters in the world.

I think of Africa,
of the tragedy of Darfur in Sudan,
of Côte d'Ivoire and of the Great Lakes region.
With great apprehension
I follow the situation in Iraq.
And how can I fail to look
with anxious concern,
but also invincible confidence,
towards that land of which you are a son?

Everywhere peace is needed!
You, prince of true peace,
help us to understand
that the only way to build peace
is to flee in horror from evil
and to pursue goodness,
always and with courage.
Men and women of good will,
of every people on the earth,
come with trust to the crib of the Savior!
"He who bestows the Kingdom of heaven
does not take away human kingdoms"
(cf. *Hymn for Vespers of Epiphany*).
Hasten to meet him;
he comes to teach us
the way of truth, peace and love.

Message "Urbi et Orbi"
Christmas 2004

Open Wide the
Doors to Christ

What is the truth? One day Jesus said: "I am the way, and the truth and the life" (Jn 14:6). Thus, the correct formulation of the question is not "*what* is the truth?" but "*who* is the truth?"

This is the question that men and women of the third millennium are also asking themselves. Dear brothers and sisters, we cannot keep silent about the answer, because we know it! The truth is Jesus Christ, who came into the world to reveal to us and give to us the Father's love. We are called to witness to this truth by our words and especially by our lives!

Homily, 6 June 2004

There is no contradiction between faith and reason, as the experience of the holy Magi shows. They reached Bethlehem using both these dimensions of the human spirit: intelligence that scrutinizes signs, and faith that leads to adoration of the mystery. To face the long and grueling journey in search of the Messiah, reason did not suffice; in order to reach their goal, the Magi also needed faith in the sign of the star. The hope and ardent longing of the Magi were not in vain. They sought the infant Jesus in Bethlehem and once they had found him, their minds needed faith in order to recognize that the humble Son of man was the Messiah, awaited and foretold by the prophets throughout the Old Testament.

Message on the Occasion of the
Vigil of Prayer, Third European
University Day, 5 March 2005

Filled with emotion, our thoughts go back to the enthusiasm of that first "yes" spoken on the day of our priestly ordination. To the One who was calling us to work for his Kingdom we replied: "Here I am!" We must say it again every day, knowing that we are sent in a special way, *in persona Christi*, to serve the community of the saved.

Homily, Holy Thursday Chrism Mass
8 April 2004

The gift and mystery we priests have received is truly extraordinary…. The Christian people want to see us first and foremost as men of prayer. What we say and the way we act must enable those who meet us to experience God's faithful and merciful love.

Homily, Holy Thursday Chrism Mass
8 April 2004

In the Eucharist Jesus thanks the Father with us and for us. How could this thanksgiving of Jesus fail to shape the life of a priest? He knows that he must cultivate a constant sense of gratitude for the many gifts he has received in the course of his life, in particular for the gift of faith, which it is his task to proclaim, and for the gift of the priesthood, which consecrates him totally to the service of the kingdom of God. We have our crosses to bear — and we are certainly not the only ones! — but the gifts we have received are so great that we cannot fail to sing from the depths of our hearts our own *Magnificat*.

Letter to Priests, Holy Thursday 2005

Every time we celebrate the Eucharist, the remembrance of Christ in his Paschal Mystery leads to the desire for a full and definitive encounter with him. We live in expectation of his coming! In priestly spirituality, this expectation must be lived out through pastoral charity, which impels us to live in the midst of God's people, so as to direct their path and nourish their hope. This task requires from the priest an interior attitude similar to that of the apostle Paul: "Forgetting what lies behind and straining forward to what lies ahead, I press on towards the goal" (Phil 3:13–14). The priest is someone who, despite the passing of years, continues to radiate youthfulness, spreading it almost contagiously among those he meets along the way. His secret lies in his passion for Christ.

Letter to Priests, Holy Thursday 2005

In a certain sense, when he says the words "Take and eat," the priest must learn to apply them also to himself, and to speak them with truth and generosity. His life has true meaning if he is able to offer himself as a gift, placing himself at the disposal of the community.

Letter to Priests, Holy Thursday 2005

Seen in this way, the special task entrusted to Peter and his successors becomes crystal clear. The Petrine ministry is essentially a service to the unity of the Church. "You are Peter, and on this rock I will build my church" (Mt 16:18). This promise of the Lord is echoed by those other comforting words of his: "I have prayed for you [Simon] that your faith may not fail; and when you have turned again, strengthen your brethren" (Lk 22: 32).

Angelus, 20 February 2005

Today, I am speaking to you from the Agostino Gemelli Polyclinic, where for several days I have been cared for with loving concern by doctors, nurses and health-care personnel, whom I warmly thank.

Dear brothers and sisters and those in every corner of the earth who are close to me, I express my thanks for your sincere and heartfelt affection, which I have felt with special intensity these days.

I assure you, one and all, of my gratitude, which I express in constant prayer to the Lord for your intentions, as well as for the needs of the Church and the great world causes. Thus I continue to serve the Church and the whole of humanity, even here in the hospital among other sick persons, whom I am thinking of with affection.

Angelus, 6 February 2005

Our age feels a deep yearning for peace. The Church, a credible sign and instrument of Christ's peace, must always strive to overcome the divisions between Christians and thereby become increasingly a witness of the peace that Christ offers to the world.

Homily, 13 November 2004

The desire for unity is spreading and becoming deeper, affecting new areas and situations and giving rise to a proliferation of works, initiatives and reflections. Recently, too, the Lord permitted his disciples to establish important contacts through dialogue and collaboration. The pain of our separation is more and more acutely felt as we face the challenges of a world that expects a clear and unanimous Gospel witness on the part of all who believe in Christ.

General Audience, 19 January 2005

We no longer consider other Christians as distant or strangers, but see them as brothers and sisters....

We are grateful to God to see that in recent years many of the faithful across the world have been moved by an ardent desire for the unity of all Christians. I warmly thank those who have made themselves instruments of the Spirit and have worked and prayed for this process of rapprochement and reconciliation.

Homily, 13 November 2004

There is no true ecumenism without inner conversion and the purification of memory, without holiness of life in conformity with the Gospel, and above all without intense and assiduous prayer that echoes the prayer of Jesus.

Homily, 13 November 2004

I would like to express special gratitude for the closeness of believers of other religions, Jews and Muslims in particular. Some of them have wanted to come and pray here at the hospital. This is a comforting sign to me for which I thank God.

Angelus from the Gemelli Polyclinic
6 March 2005

Help us, Jesus, to understand that in order to *do* in your Church ... we must first learn to *be*, that is, to stay with you in adoration, in your sweet company. Authentic, effective and true apostolic action can come only from intimate communion with you.

Message to the Young People
of Rome and Lazio, 17 March 2005

To live the Eucharist it is necessary to spend much time in adoration before the Blessed Sacrament, something I myself experience every day, drawing from it strength, consolation and assistance.

Message for World Mission Day
19 April 2004

It is significant that the two disciples on the road to Emmaus, duly prepared by our Lord's words, recognized him at table through the simple gesture of the breaking of bread. When minds are enlightened and hearts are enkindled, signs begin to speak. The Eucharist unfolds in a dynamic context of signs containing a rich and luminous message. Through these signs the mystery opens up, in a way, before the eyes of the believer.

Apostolic Letter
Mane nobiscum Domine (II, 14)
7 October 2004

Dear brothers and sisters, we must allow the needs of our many brothers and sisters to speak to us. We cannot close our hearts to their pleas for help. Nor can we forget that "one does not live by bread alone" (cf. Mt 4:4). We are in need of the "living bread which came down from heaven" (Jn 6:51). Jesus is this bread. Nourishing ourselves on him means welcoming God's life itself (cf. Jn 10:10) and opening ourselves to the logic of love and sharing.

Address, Opening of the Year of the Eucharist
17 October 2004

Christ, "the living bread that came down from heaven" (Jn 6:51), is the only one who can satisfy the hunger of human beings of every time and in every corner of the earth.

However, he does not want to do this on his own, so he involves the disciples, as he did in the multiplication of the loaves: "Taking the five loaves and the two fish, he looked up to heaven, and blessed and broke them and gave them to the disciples to set before the crowd" (Lk 9:16). This miraculous sign is a symbol of the greatest mystery of love which is renewed every day at Mass.

Homily, 10 June 2004

This bread of eternal life is Christ, the wellspring of our hope and the source of love from which gifts of justice, forgiveness and peace are constantly poured out upon the world. Let us experience the riches of this mystery, dear friends, especially by taking part in holy Mass on Sundays, which for Christians is the center and culmination of the week.

Address, 8 January 2005

When the ecclesial community celebrates the Eucharist, especially on Sunday the Day of the Lord, it experiences in the light of the faith the value of the encounter with the risen Christ and is ever more aware that the sacrifice of the Eucharist is "for all" (cf. Mt 26:28). We who nourish ourselves with the Body and Blood of the crucified and risen Lord, cannot keep this gift for ourselves; on the contrary we must share it. Passionate love for Christ leads to courageous proclamation of Christ; proclamation which, with martyrdom, becomes a supreme offering of love for God and for mankind. The Eucharist leads us to be generous evangelizers, actively committed to building a more just and fraternal world.

Message Prepared for World
Mission Day 2005
Released 15 April 2005

Mystery of light! The human heart, burdened with sin, often bewildered, weary and tried by suffering of all kinds, has need of light. The world needs light in the difficult quest for a peace that seems remote, at the beginning of a millennium overwhelmed and humiliated by violence, terrorism and war.

The Eucharist is light! In the Word of God constantly proclaimed, in the bread and wine that have become the Body and Blood of Christ, it is really he, the risen Lord, who opens minds and hearts and makes us recognize him, as he made the two disciples at Emmaus recognize him in the breaking of the bread (cf. Lk 24:35). In this convivial gesture we relive the sacrifice of the Cross, we experience God's infinite love, we feel called to spread Christ's light among the men and women of our time.

Address, Opening of the Year of the Eucharist
17 October 2004

Mane nobiscum, Domine! Like the two disciples in the Gospel, we implore you, Lord Jesus, *stay with us!*

Divine Wayfarer, expert in our ways and reader of our hearts, do not leave us prisoners to the evening shadows.

Sustain us in our weariness, forgive our sins and direct our steps on the path of goodness.

Address, Opening of the Year of the Eucharist
17 October 2004

Stay with us, Lord! (cf. Lk 24:29).
With these words,
the disciples on the road to Emmaus
invited the mysterious Wayfarer
to stay with them, as the sun was setting
on that first day of the week
when the incredible had occurred.
According to his promise, Christ had risen;
but they did not yet know this.
Nevertheless, the words spoken
by the Wayfarer along the road
made their hearts burn within them.
So they said to him: "Stay with us."
Seated around the supper table,
they recognized him in the breaking of bread
— and suddenly he vanished.
There remained in front of them
the broken bread;
there echoed in their hearts the gentle sound
of his words.

Dear brothers and sisters,
the Word and the Bread of the Eucharist,
the mystery and the gift of Easter,
remain down the centuries
as a constant memorial
of the Passion, Death and Resurrection

of Christ!
On this Easter day,
together with all Christians
throughout the world,
we too repeat those words:
Jesus, crucified and risen, stay with us!
Stay with us, faithful friend
and sure support for humanity
on its journey through history!
Living Word of the Father,
give hope and trust to all who are searching
for the true meaning of their lives.
Bread of eternal life, nourish those who hunger
for truth, freedom, justice and peace.

Stay with us, Living Word of the Father,
and teach us words and deeds of peace:
peace for our world
consecrated by your blood
and drenched in the blood
of so many innocent victims;
peace for the countries
of the Middle East and Africa,
where so much blood continues to be shed;
peace for all of humanity,
still threatened by fratricidal wars.
Stay with us, Bread of eternal life,

broken and distributed to those at table.
Give us also the strength to show
generous solidarity towards the multitudes
who are even today suffering and dying
from poverty and hunger,
decimated by fatal epidemics
or devastated by immense natural disasters.
By the power of your Resurrection,
may they too become sharers in new life.

We, the men and women
of the third millennium,
we too need you, risen Lord!
Stay with us now and until the end of time.
Grant that the material progress of peoples
may never obscure the spiritual values
which are the soul of their civilization.
Sustain us, we pray, on our journey.
In you do we believe, in you do we hope,
for you alone have the words of eternal life
(cf. Jn 6:68).

Message "Urbi et Orbi"
Easter 2005

As a gift to humanity, which sometimes seems bewildered and overwhelmed by the power of evil, selfishness and fear, the risen Lord offers his love, which pardons, reconciles and reopens hearts to hope. It is a love that converts hearts and gives peace. How much the world needs to understand and accept divine mercy!

Lord, who reveal the Father's love by your death and Resurrection, we believe in you and confidently repeat to you today: Jesus, I trust in you, have mercy upon us and upon the whole world.

Regina Caeli, Feast of Divine Mercy
3 April 2005

You've Come to See Me, and I Thank You

Twenty years ago, at the end of the Holy Year of the Redemption, I presented the large wooden cross of that Jubilee to the young people....

Since then the cross has continued to travel to many countries in preparation for the Word Youth Days. During its pilgrimages it has crossed continents. Like a torch passed hand to hand, it was transported from country to country; it has become a luminous sign of the trust that animates the young generations of the third millennium.

Homily, 4 April 2004

I recall with fondness my meetings with young people…. These meetings have given me a great hope, which I wish to share with you today. Let Mary be your teacher, and you will bring a fresh breath of optimism to the world.

Angelus, 15 August 2004

Dear young people, I realize more and more how providential and prophetic it was that this very day, Palm Sunday and the Passion of the Lord, should have become your day. This feast possesses a special grace, that of joy united to the cross, which sums up in itself the Christian mystery.

Today, I say to you: continue unflaggingly on the journey on which you have set out in order to be witnesses everywhere of the glorious cross of Christ. Do not be afraid! May the joy of the Lord, crucified and risen, be your strength, and may Mary most holy always be beside you.

Angelus, 20 March 2005

Of course, the message that the cross communicates is not easy to understand in our day and age, in which material well-being and conveniences are offered and sought as priority values. But you, dear young people, do not be afraid to proclaim the Gospel of the cross in every circumstance. Do not be afraid to swim against the tide!

Homily, 4 April 2004

My dear young people, do not yield to false illusions and passing fads, which so frequently leave behind a tragic spiritual vacuum! Reject the seduction of wealth, consumerism and the subtle violence sometimes used by the mass media.

Worshiping the true God is an authentic act of resistance to all forms of idolatry. Worship Christ. He is the rock on which to build your future and a world of greater justice and solidarity.

Message Prepared for the 20th World
Youth Day, 6 August 2005

Listening to Christ and worshiping him leads us to make courageous choices, to make what are sometimes heroic decisions. Jesus is demanding, because he wishes our genuine happiness…. When we meet Christ and accept his Gospel, life changes and we are driven to communicate our experience to others.

Message Prepared for the 20th World Youth Day, 6 August 2005

Music, like all the languages of art, brings men and women closer to God, who has prepared for those who love him "what no eye has seen, nor ear heard, nor the heart of man conceived" (1 Cor 2: 9). But at the same time, art can sometimes be the vehicle for a concept of the human being, of love or of happiness that does not correspond to the truth of God's plan…. It is also up to you, dear young people, to renew the languages of art and culture.

Message to the Participants
Annual International Congress UNIV, 2005

"Opening their treasures, they offered him gifts, gold and frankincense and myrrh" (Mt 2:11). The gifts that the Magi offered the Messiah symbolized true worship. With gold, they emphasized his royal Godhead; with incense, they acknowledged him as priest of the New Covenant; by offering him myrrh, they celebrated the prophet who would shed his own blood to reconcile humanity with the Father.

My dear young people, you too offer to the Lord the gold of your lives, namely, your freedom to follow him out of love by responding faithfully to his call; let the incense of your fervent prayer rise up to him, in praise of his glory; offer him your myrrh, that is, your grateful affection for him, true man, who loved us to the point of dying as a criminal on Golgotha.

Message Prepared for the 20th World
Youth Day, 6 August 2005

The time has come for preparing young generations of apostles who are not afraid to proclaim the Gospel. It is essential for every baptized person to pass from a faith of habit to a mature faith that is expressed in clear, convinced and courageous personal choices.

Homily, 6 June 2004

In the Gospel, Jesus proclaims: "Blessed are the peacemakers" (Mt 5: 9). These little ones can also be peacemakers! They too must train themselves in dialogue and must learn "to defeat evil with good" (cf. Rom 12:21)….

This lifestyle is not created from nothing; it requires education, beginning in infancy. This education comes from wise teachings and above all from sound models in the family, in school and in every part of society….

Let us pray to Mary, Queen of Peace, that she may help young people, who desire peace so much, to become its courageous and tenacious builders.

Angelus, 30 January 2005

Dear young people, may you always be motivated by the desire to discover the truth of your lives. May faith and reason be the two wings that bear you aloft towards Christ, the truth about God and the truth about man. In Christ you will find peace and joy.

Message on the Occasion
of the Vigil of Prayer
Third European University Day
5 March 2005

O Jesus in the Eucharist, to you I entrust the young people of the whole world, with their sentiments, their affections and their projects. I present them to you through the hands of Mary, your mother and ours.

Jesus, who offered yourself to the Father: love them!

Jesus, who offered yourself to the Father: heal their spiritual wounds!

Jesus, who offered yourself to the Father: help them to adore you in truth and bless them. Now and forever.

Amen!

Message to the Young People
of Rome and Lazio, 17 March 2005

Totus Tuus

To Mary, Mother of the Church, I once again entrust myself: *Totus tuus!* May she help us to fulfill God's will in every moment of life.

Angelus, 27 February 2005

Kneeling here, before the grotto of Massabielle, I feel deeply that I have reached the goal of my pilgrimage.

Grotto of Massabielle, 14 August 2004
(Pope John Paul's last trip abroad)

Christianity is truly a fountain of life, and Mary is the first guardian of this fountain. She points it out to all people, inviting them to renounce their pride and learn humility, so that they can draw from the mercy of her Son and thus work together for the dawn of the civilization of love.

Angelus, 15 August 2004

"In those days Mary arose and went with haste into the hill country..." (Lk 1:39). The words of the Gospel story have once more brought before the eyes of our hearts the young maiden of Nazareth as she makes her way to the "city of Judah" where her kinswoman Elizabeth lived, in order to be of help to her.

What strikes us about Mary is above all her loving concern for her elderly relative. Hers is a practical love, one which is not limited to words of understanding but is deeply and personally involved in giving help. The Blessed Virgin does not merely give her cousin something of herself; *she gives her whole self*, asking nothing in return. Mary understood perfectly that the gift she received from God is more than a *privilege*; it is a *duty* which obliges her to serve others with the selflessness proper to love.

Homily, 15 August 2004

The *Magnificat* is followed by silence. Nothing is said to us about the three months that Mary stayed with her kinswoman Elizabeth. Yet perhaps we are told the most important thing: that *goodness works quietly*, the power of love is expressed in the unassuming quietness of daily service.

Homily, 15 August 2004

By her words and her silence the Virgin Mary stands before us as a model for our pilgrim way. It is not an easy way…. But evil and death *will not have the last word!* Mary confirms this by her whole life, for she is a living witness of the victory of Christ, our Passover.

Homily, 15 August 2004

To you, Immaculate Virgin, predestined by God above every other creature to be the advocate of grace and model of holiness for his people, today in a special way I entrust to you again the whole Church.

May you guide your children on their pilgrimage of faith, making them ever more obedient and faithful to the Word of God.

May you accompany every Christian on the path of conversion and holiness, in the fight against sin and in the search for true beauty that is always an impression and reflection of divine beauty.

May you obtain peace and salvation for all peoples. May the eternal Father, who desired you to be the immaculate Mother of the Redeemer, also renew in our time, through you, the miracles of his merciful love.

Homily, 8 December 2004

Appearing in this grotto, Mary entrusted her message to a young girl, as if to emphasize the special mission of women in our own time, tempted as it is by materialism and secularism: to be in today's society a witness of those essential values which are seen only with the eyes of the heart. To you, women, falls the task of being sentinels of the Invisible!

Homily, 15 August 2004

The visit of the Virgin Mary which Lucia, as a little girl, received at Fatima in 1917 together with her cousins Francisco and Jacinta, was the beginning of a unique mission to which she remained faithful to the end of her days. Sister Lucia bequeaths to us an example of great fidelity to the Lord and joyful attachment to his divine will.

I recall with emotion my several meetings with her and the bonds of our spiritual friendship that grew stronger with time. I have always felt supported by the daily gift of her prayers, especially during the most difficult moments of trial and suffering. May the Lord reward her abundantly for her great and hidden service to the Church.

I like to think that it was the Blessed Virgin, the same one whom Sister Lucia saw at Fatima so many years ago, who welcomed her on her pious departure from earth to heaven.

Letter to the Bishop of Coimbra
14 February 2005

Hail Mary,
poor and humble woman,
blessed by the Most High!
Virgin of hope,
promise of a new era,
we join in your song of praise,
to celebrate the Lord's mercies,
to proclaim the coming of the Kingdom
and the full liberation of humanity.

Lourdes, 14 August 2004

Hail Mary,
lowly handmaid of the Lord,
glorious Mother of Christ!
Faithful virgin,
holy dwelling-place of the Word,
teach us to persevere
in listening to the Word,
and to be docile to the voice of the Spirit,
attentive to his promptings
in the depths of our conscience
and to his manifestations
in the events of history.

Lourdes, 14 August 2004

Hail Mary,
woman of sorrows,
mother of the living!
Virgin spouse beneath the Cross,
the new Eve,
be our guide along the paths of the world.
Teach us to experience and to spread
the love of Christ,
to stand with you
before the innumerable crosses
on which your Son is still crucified.

Lourdes, 14 August 2004

Hail Mary,
woman of faith,
first of the disciples!
Virgin Mother of the Church,
help us always to give an account
of the hope that is in us,
with trust in people's goodness
and in the Father's love.
Teach us to build up the world
beginning from within:
in the depths of silence and prayer,
in the joy of fraternal love,
in the unique fruitfulness of the cross.

Holy Mary,
mother of believers,
our Lady of Lourdes,
pray for us.

Lourdes, 14 August 2004

Finally, our Lady of Lourdes has a message for everyone. *Be men and women of freedom!* But remember: human freedom is a freedom wounded by sin. It is a freedom which itself needs to be set free. Christ is its liberator; he is the one who "for freedom has set us free" (cf. Gal 5:1). Defend that freedom!

Dear friends, in this we know we can count on Mary, who, since she never yielded to sin, is the only creature who is perfectly free. I entrust you to her. Walk beside Mary as you journey towards the complete fulfillment of your humanity!

Homily, 15 August 2004

Amen

Here at this Grotto of Massabielle, I wish first of all to greet the sick who come in ever greater numbers to this shrine, those who have accompanied them, their caregivers and their families.

I am here with you, dear brothers and sisters, as a pilgrim to our Lady. I make my own your prayers and your hopes. With you I share a time of life marked by physical suffering, yet not for that reason any less fruitful in God's wondrous plan.

> Greeting to the Sick at Lourdes
> 14 August 2004

Health is not, of course, an absolute good. It is not such especially when it is taken to be merely physical well-being, mythicized to the point of limiting or neglecting higher goods....

Properly understood, health nevertheless continues to be one of the most important goods for which we all have a clear responsibility, to the point that it can be sacrificed only in order to attain higher goods, as is sometimes demanded in the service of God, one's family, one's neighbor and the whole of society.

Letter to the President of the Pontifical
Academy for Life, 19 February 2005

The passing years make us feel ever more keenly the need for divine and human help.

Address to the Roman Curia
21 December 2004

"For what man can learn the counsel of God?" (Wis 9:13). The question asked in the book of Wisdom has one answer. Only the Son of God, made man for our salvation in the virginal womb of Mary, can reveal God's design to us. Jesus alone knows which is the path that leads to "wisdom of heart" (cf. Responsorial Psalm) and to peace and salvation.

And what is this way? He has given us the answer in today's Gospel. It is the *way of the Cross*. His words are clear: "Whoever does not bear his own cross and come after me, cannot be my disciple" (Lk 14:27).

Carrying the cross, following Jesus, means being prepared to make any sacrifice for love of him. It means not putting anything or anyone before him, not even those you love the most, not even your own life.

Homily, 5 September 2004

The adoration of the Cross directs us to a commitment that we cannot shirk. It is the mission that St. Paul expressed in these words: "In my flesh I complete what is lacking in Christ's afflictions for the sake of his body, that is, the Church" (Col 1: 24). I also offer my sufferings so that God's plan may be completed and his Word spread among the peoples.

Message to the Participants
in the Way of the Cross
Good Friday, 25 March 2005

On this memorial day of Christ's crucifixion, I look at the cross with you in adoration, repeating the words of the liturgy: *O crux, ave spes unica!* Hail, O cross, our only hope, give us patience and courage and obtain peace for the world!

Message to the Participants
in the Way of the Cross
Good Friday, 25 March 2005

The penitential season of Lent that we are living helps us to understand better the value of suffering, which in one way or another touches us all. It is in looking at Christ and following him with patient trust that we are able to understand how every human form of suffering contains a divine promise of salvation and joy. I would like this message of comfort and hope to reach everyone, especially those who are going through difficult moments and those who suffer in body and in spirit.

Angelus, 27 February 2005

I always feel in need of your help before the Lord in order to carry out the mission that Jesus has entrusted to me.

With the rite of ashes, we have begun Lent, the liturgical season that reminds us every year of a fundamental truth: we do not enter eternal life without bearing our cross in union with Christ. We do not attain happiness and peace without courageously facing inner combat. This combat is won with the weapons of penance: prayer, fasting and works of mercy. All this must be done in secret, without hypocrisy, in a spirit of sincere love for God and our brothers and sisters.

Angelus, 13 February 2005

You know that adhering to Christ is a demanding decision. It is not by chance that Jesus speaks of the cross. But he straightaway explains: "after me." These are the important words. We are not alone in carrying our cross; he walks ahead of us, showing us the way with the light of his example and the power of his love.

Homily, 5 September 2004

In dying on the cross, Christ, the man of sorrows, brought the Father's plan of love to fulfillment and redeemed the world. My dear sick people, if you join your suffering to the suffering of Christ, you will be his privileged cooperators in the salvation of souls. This is your task in the Church, which is always deeply aware of the role and value of illness enlightened by faith. And so your suffering is never wasted! Indeed, it is valuable, for it is a mysterious but real sharing in the saving mission of the Son of God.

Message to the Sick, 11 February 2005

Dear brothers and sisters who are sick, how I would like to embrace each and every one of you with affection, to tell you how close I am to you and how much I support you. I now do so in spirit, entrusting you to the maternal love of the Mother of the Lord.

Greeting to the Sick at Lourdes
14 August 2004

The flow of sick and suffering people to the feet of the Blessed Virgin is a constant exhortation to entrust ourselves to Christ and his heavenly Mother, who never abandon those who turn to them in moments of suffering and trial.

Message to the Sick, 11 February 2005

There is *no greater love* than that of the cross; there is *no truer freedom* than that of love; there is *no more complete brotherhood* than that which is born from the cross of Jesus.

Homily, 5 September 2004

We must become accustomed to thinking confidently about the mystery of death, so that the definitive encounter with God may take place in an atmosphere of inner peace, in the awareness that the one who will receive it is the One who knit us "in our mother's womb" (cf. Ps 139:13b) and willed us "in his image and likeness" (cf. Gn 1:26).

Message for Lent, 2005

Spiritual Testament

(Testament of 6 March 1979 and later additions)

Totus Tuus ego sum

In the Name of the Most Holy Trinity.
Amen.

"Watch, therefore, for you do not know on what day your Lord is coming" (Mt 24:42) — these words remind me of the last call that will come at whatever time the Lord desires. I want to follow him and I want all that is part of my earthly life to prepare me for this moment. I do not know when it will come, but I place this moment, like all other things, in the hands of the Mother of my Master: *Totus Tuus.* In these same motherly hands I leave everything and everyone with whom my life and my vocation have brought me into contact. In these hands I above all leave the Church, and also my nation and all humanity. I thank everyone. I ask forgiveness of everyone. I also ask for prayers, so that God's mercy may prove greater than my own weakness and unworthiness.

During the spiritual exercises I reread the testament of the Holy Father Paul VI. It was reading it that gave me the incentive to write this testament.

I leave no possessions of which it will be necessary to dispose. As for the things I use every day, I ask that they be distributed as seems appropriate. Let my personal notes be burned. I ask that Father Stanisław see to this, and I thank him for his help and collaboration, so understanding for so many years. On the other hand, I leave all my other "thank you's" in my heart before God himself, because it is difficult to express them.

With regard to my funeral, I repeat the instructions that were given by the Holy Father Paul VI (*here a note in the margin says:* burial in the ground and not in a sarcophagus, 13 March 1992). Let the College of Cardinals and my fellow citizens decide on the place.

"apud Dominum misericordia
et copiosa apud Eum redemptio"

John Paul PP. II

Rome, 6 March 1979

After my death I ask for Holy Masses and prayers

5 February 1990

******

(Undated Page)

I express the most profound trust that, in spite of all my weakness, the Lord will grant me every grace necessary to face, in accordance with his will, any task, test or suffering that he sees fit to ask of his servant during his life. I am also confident that he will never let me fail through some attitude I may have — words, deeds or omissions — in my obligations to this holy Petrine See.

******

24 February – 1 March 1980

Also during these spiritual exercises I reflected on the truth of the priesthood of Christ in view of that passing which the moment of death is for each one of us. The resurrection of Christ is an eloquent [*above this word was added* "decisive"] sign of the departure from this world for rebirth in the other, future world.

I have therefore read the draft of my testament as it was recorded last year, also written during the spiritual exercises. I compared it with the testament of my great predecessor and father, Paul VI, with his sublime testimony on the death of a Christian and a pope — and I reminded myself of the matters mentioned in the draft of 6 March 1979, prepared by me (in a somewhat makeshift manner).

Today I would like to add only this: that everyone keep the prospect of death in mind and be ready to go before the Lord and Judge — and at the same time Redeemer and Father. So I keep this continually in mind, entrusting that decisive moment to the Mother of Christ and of the Church — to the mother of my hope.

The times we are living in are unspeakably difficult and disturbing. The Church's journey has also become difficult and stressful, a characteristic proof of these times, both for the faithful and for pastors. In some countries (as, for example, those I read about during the spiritual exercises), the Church finds herself in a period of persecution no less evil than the persecutions of the early centuries, indeed worse, because of the degree of ruthlessness and hatred. *Sanguis martyrum — semen christianorum* ["The blood of martyrs is the seed of Christians" (Tertullian)]. And in addition to this, so many innocent people disappear, even in this country in which we live....

I would like once again to entrust myself entirely to the Lord's grace. He himself will decide when and how I am to end my earthly life and my pastoral ministry. In life and in death [I am] *Totus Tuus* through Mary Immaculate. I hope, in accepting my death already now, that Christ will give me the grace I need for the final passover, that is, [my] Pasch. I also hope that he will make it benefit this more important cause I seek to serve: the salvation of men and women, the preservation of the human family and, within it, all nations and peoples (among them, my heart turns particularly to my earthly homeland), useful for the people he has specially entrusted to me, for the matter of the Church and for the glory of God himself.

I do not want to add anything to what I wrote a year ago — except to express this readiness and at the same time this trust, which these spiritual exercises have once again inspired in me.

John Paul II

******

5 March 1982

In the course of the spiritual exercises this year I read (several times) the text of my testament of 6 March 1979. Although I still consider it as temporary (not definitive) I am leaving it in its present form. I am not (for the moment) changing anything, nor am I adding anything to the arrangements it contains.

The attack on my life on 13 May 1981 in some way confirmed the accurateness of the words I wrote during the spiritual exercises in 1980 (24 February – 1 March).

I feel so much more deeply that I am totally in God's hands — and I remain continuously available to my Lord, entrusting myself to him through his Immaculate Mother *(Totus Tuus)*.

John Paul PP. II

P.S.

In connection with the last sentence of my testament of 6 March 1979 ("Let the College of Cardinals and my fellow citizens decide on the place, that is, the place of the funeral") — I explain what I have in mind, namely, the metropolitan of Krakow or the General Council of the Polish Bishops' Conference. Meanwhile, I ask the College of Cardinals to do their best to satisfy any requests of those listed above.

******

1 March 1985

Once again, with regard to the expression "the College of Cardinals and my fellow citizens." The College of Cardinals is under no obligation to consult my fellow citizens on this matter; it may do so, however, if for some reason it should deem it appropriate.

JPII

******

The spiritual exercises in the Jubilee Year 2000

(12 – 18 March)

[for the testament]

1. When the conclave of cardinals chose John Paul II on 16 October 1978, Cardinal Stefan Wyszynski, the primate of Poland, said to me: *"The task of the new Pope* will be *to lead the Church into the Third Millennium."* I do not know if I am repeating the sentence exactly as he said it, but this was at least the sense of what I heard him say at the time. These words were spoken by the man who went down in history as the primate of the millennium. A great primate. I witnessed his mission, his total confidence, his struggles and his triumph. "When victory is won, it will be a victory through Mary." The primate of the millennium was fond of repeating these words of his predecessor, Cardinal August Hlond.

Thus I was in some way prepared for the task presented to me that day, 16 October 1978. As I write these words, *the Great Jubilee of the Year 2000* is already a reality that is taking place. On the night of 24 December 1999 the symbolic great jubilee door in the Basilica of St. Peter was opened, and subsequently that of St. John Lateran, then that of St. Mary Major on New Year's Day, and on 19 January the door of the Basilica of St Paul Outside-the-Walls. Particularly the latter event, because of its ecumenical character, was imprinted indelibly on memories.

2. As the Great Jubilee of the Year 2000 continues, the twentieth century closes behind us and the twenty-first century unfolds, from one day to the next. In accordance with the designs of Providence, I have been granted to live in the difficult century that is retreating into the past, and now in the year in which I have reached my 80s (*"octogesima adveniens"*), I must ask myself *whether the time has come to say with Simeon of the Bible, "Nunc dimittis."*

On 13 May 1981, the day of the attack on the Pope during the general audience in St. Peter's Square, divine Providence miraculously saved me from death. He himself, who is the one Lord of life and death, extended this life of mine, and in a certain way restored it to me. Ever since that moment it has belonged even more to him. I hope he will help me to recognize how long I must continue this service to which he called me on 16 October 1978. I ask him to be pleased to call me whenever he himself wishes. "If we live, we live to the Lord, and if we die, we die to the Lord; so then ... we are the Lord's" (cf. Rom 14:8). I hope that for as long as I am given to carry out the Petrine service in the Church, God in his mercy will grant me the necessary strength for this service.

3. As I do every year during the spiritual exercises, I read the testament that I wrote on

6 March 1979. I continue to keep the instructions it contains. What was added then, and also during the subsequent spiritual retreats, reflects the difficult and tense general situation that marked the 1980s. After autumn of the year 1989, this situation changed. The final decade of the last century was free of the previous tensions; this does not mean that it did not bring new problems and difficulties. In a special way *may divine Providence be praised for this*, that the period known as the Cold War ended *without violent nuclear conflict;* the risk of it had been threatening the world in the previous period.

4. As I stand on the threshold of the third millennium, *"in medio Ecclesiae,"* I would like once again to express my *gratitude to the Holy Spirit* for *the great gift of the Second Vatican Council,* to which, together with the whole Church — and especially with the whole episcopate — I feel indebted. I am convinced that the new generations will be able, for a long time to come, to draw from the treasures that this twentieth-century Council has lavished upon us. As a bishop who took part in the Council from the first to the last day, I desire to entrust this great patrimony to all who are and will be called in the future to put it into practice. For my part, I thank the eternal Pastor who has enabled me to serve this very great cause in the course of all the years of my pontificate.

"In medio Ecclesiae"... From the very first years of my service as a bishop — thanks to the Council — I was granted to *experience the fraternal communion of the episcopate.* As a priest of the Archdiocese of Krakow I had experienced the fraternal communion of the presbyterate — the Council opened a new dimension of this experience.

5. *How many people* I would have to list! The Lord God has probably called the majority of them to himself. As for those who are still here, may the words of this testament recall them, everyone and everywhere, wherever they may happen to be.

In the course of the more than twenty years that I have been carrying out the Petrine service *"in medio Ecclesiae," I have experienced the benevolent and most especially the fruitful collaboration of so many* cardinals, archbishops and bishops, so many priests and so many consecrated persons — brothers and sisters — finally, of so very many lay people, in the Curia and in the Vicariate of the Diocese of Rome, as well as outside these places.

How could I not embrace with grateful memories all the episcopal conferences in the world with whom I met in the course of their visits *ad limina Apostolorum!* How could I also fail to remember so many Christian brothers and sisters who were not Catholics! And the Rabbi of Rome and likewise all the representatives of non-Christian religions, not to mention all the representatives of the worlds of culture, science, politics and the media!

6. As the end of my earthly life draws close, I think back to its beginning, to my parents, to my brother and my sister (whom I never knew, for she died before I was born), to the parish in Wadowice where I was baptized, to that city of my youth, to my peers, my classmates of both sexes in elementary school, high school and the university, until the time of the occupation when I worked as a laborer, and later the parish in Niegowic, St. Florian's Parish in Krakow, the university chaplaincy, the places ... all the places ... Krakow and Rome ... the persons who were especially entrusted to me by the Lord.

I want to say just one thing to them all: "May God reward you!"

"In manus tuas, Domine, commendo spiritum meum."

17 March 2000, A.D.

Also available from New City Press:

99 Sayings
by John Paul II

On Our Pilgrimage
to Eternity
99 Sayings by John Paul II

hardcover:
1-56548-198-4, ribbon, 112 pp.
softcover:
1-56548-230-1, 112 pp.

The pontificate of the first non-Italian since the sixteenth century has left a lasting imprint on the church and on the world. John Paul II has offered clear guidance for Roman Catholics, Christians of other denominations, members of other great religions, and innumerable others of good will. The moving selections from his writings contained here speak of his central creed: the good news of Jesus, humanity's friend and savior, and his relevance to our own life and times.

"The 99 Words to Live By series has added impressive quotations from Pope John Paul II to its popular inspirational and gift line.... The book is a pithy reminder of how much society owes to this pope."

Prairie Messenger